FEELINGS

Stories for Assembly and P.S.E.

Gordon Aspland

SOUTHGATE

Copyright © Gordon Aspland 1994
Copyright © Illustrations Jenny Bidgood

First published 1994 by Southgate Publishers Ltd
Reprinted 1995

Southgate Publishers Ltd
Glebe House, Church Street, Crediton, Devon EX17 2AF

Printed and bound in Great Britain by Short Run Press, Exeter, Devon

British Library Cataloguing in Publication Data
A CIP catalogue record for this book is available from the British Library.

ISBN 1–85741–091–2

CONTENTS

FEELINGS
Introduction

In writing *Feelings* I have tried to deal with issues that affect many children. Issues such as fairness, friendship, responsibility, stealing and respect can be addressed as relevant to the primary school child. These stories are designed to stimulate children to think about and then perhaps discuss their own feelings and how they would cope in certain situations. It is hoped that through this process of listening and thinking and putting views forward, then adapting them in the light of the response of others, that children will begin to understand something of their feelings about themselves and other people.

There are two types of story in the book. One is based on conflict, usually with somebody doing something wrong, such as in 'The Ice-blue Porsche' or 'The Long Wait'. The other type of story looks at exemplars of success and how children overcome their fears to achieve in some way, such as in 'The Concert' or 'The Dog'. All the stories are based on the same group of children in the same class. By this means I hope that listeners can build up a picture of the characters and their personalities as the stories develop. They might identify with one or more of them.

The stories were written initially for my own use in collective worship, but a colleague in another school began to use them enthusiastically to support her language work in class. The quality of oral and written work she reported after she had read 'The Ice-blue Porsche' to the class was such that she asked for several more stories to use, keeping me very busy! Whether used in the classroom or in the hall, the stories allow flexibility for the teacher to use them in several contexts.

SUGGESTIONS FOR USE

In Collective Worship
This book can be picked up and the stories used just as they are by the teacher in a hurry. They take between five and fifteen minutes to read and, with a short follow-up discussion, song or hymn and prayer, or time for silent reflection, they would occupy a full assembly for collective worship of between fifteen and twenty minutes in length. More satisfactory than this *ad hoc* use is the planning of episodes from the

book into a full-term pattern of collective worship, alongside religious material from Christianity and other world faiths, so that Tuesday, say, might be the day for a visit to the world of the children in these stories, with other things happening on the other days. This would provide a coherent framework in which to set these 'broadly Christian' but essentially secular stories which would meet the requirement of the Education Reform Act that, taking a term as a whole, the collective worship must be wholly or mainly of a broadly Christian nature.

After each story I have provided questions for discussion or reflection. There is also a prayer for those schools who wish to incorporate it into their act of worship. Prayer can be introduced in an open-ended way by phrases like 'We're going to have a few quiet moments to think about ... ' or 'If you wish, share this prayer I'm going to read ... '.

As well as, or instead of, using the story in collective worship, some teachers might want to use some of the follow-up activities suggested in class.

RELIGIOUS LINKS

This book is concerned more with Personal and Social Education than with R.E. P.S.E. is no substitute for a thorough-going R.E. programme based on an R.E. Agreed Syllabus and this book makes no claim to be presenting an R.E. course or R.E. material. The Religious Links after each story are intended to link themes in the story with more explicitly religious, usually Christian, material that could be incorporated into the act of worship by the teacher if appropriate. Such links in themselves do not turn the material into R.E., for religious material is weakened when used as a tagged-on supplement or as a 'prop' for work in another subject area unless it is also dealt with fully in its own right.

In Classwork

Within the National Curriculum framework the stories might be used particularly in oral work in P.S.E. and English.

1. In pairs, the children can discuss the story. The teacher then asks one child to relate how their partner feels. This is a simple but effective way of encouraging listening as well as talking.

2. The children can be asked to write down a response to the story or how they think it should end and then discuss what they have written in a small group. A variation on this is to split the class in half. One half sits in a circle facing outwards and the other half forms a circle facing inwards, so that each is facing someone from the inner circle. The teacher can then ask questions about the story or the children's response and the children discuss in pairs. After each question, the children in the outer circle move round so that they are facing somebody new. This encourages children to talk to someone they might not normally relate to and means that the shy child may meet someone they can talk to as the outer circle moves.

3. Some stories have a natural break in the middle for questions and discussion about what happens next.

By using the Discussion/Reflection questions after each story and some of the oral work mentioned above, children can start to develop skills appropriate to P.S.E. such as: predicting outcomes from different types of behaviour; empathizing with other people's feelings; reflecting on their own behaviour and feelings; and respecting the views and feelings of others.

The sub-title of this book sums up its real intention — to provide stories for use in collective worship and P.S.E., born out of my own work with children in the upper part of the primary school. I hope it will help other teachers in their work in this area.

Gordon Aspland
1994

1
The Ice-blue Porsche

THEME: jumping to the wrong conclusions

C alvin and Tom became very good friends, but their friendship did not start well. This story tells about what happened when Calvin first arrived in Mrs Jones's class.

Tom watched the new boy come into the classroom. He looked worried and frightened, his large brown eyes staring around the room looking for a friendly face. Tom remembered his first day at school and he felt sorry for him.

"Class, this is Calvin Livingstone," announced Mrs Jones. The teacher looked around the classroom and, noticing a spare chair by Tom, said, "Tom, maybe you could look after Calvin and show him where everything is."

Calvin sat in the empty chair. He was gripping his pencil case, too scared even to put it on to the table. Tom smiled at him but couldn't say anything because they were going straight into a Maths lesson.

"Please Miss," called Tom, as he put up his hand to attract Mrs Jones's attention, "Calvin hasn't got a Maths book."

"Of course, thank you, Tom," she replied. She gave Calvin an exercise book and a worksheet. Tom showed him how they were used to setting out their work.

At playtime Tom asked Calvin if he liked playing football and, when he said he did, Tom invited him to be on his side. Calvin began to relax a bit. Tom and the other boys were very friendly towards him and said "Well done" every time he played a good shot and patted him on the back when he scored a goal. After playtime they had to write a story, first in rough using a pencil, then after it was marked for spellings they could rewrite it using a pen.

Later in the lesson Calvin noticed that most of the children were using either biros or felt-tipped pens for their rewriting. Feeling a little worried, he went up to Mrs Jones and asked, "Please Miss, can I use this fountain pen?" Mrs Jones said that he could and he returned to his seat much happier.

"That's a nice pen," remarked Tom, looking at the black and gold fountain pen.

"It was a present from my grandmother. It used to belong to my grandpa but when he died she gave it to me. They used to live in Jamaica and my grandpa worked for a very rich man. When they came to this country the rich man gave it to him as a present," explained Calvin. The ink seemed to flow like magic as he wrote. Tom looked at his own page and thought how untidy his scrawly writing in biro looked.

The week went quickly. Calvin settled into the routine and he and Tom became good friends. Tom asked him if he wanted to come and play at his house on Saturday afternoon. Calvin said he would like to but he had to check with his mother first. He telephoned Tom that evening to say he could come and he was allowed to stay for tea as well.

When Calvin arrived, Tom took him straight up to his bedroom. Calvin stood in the doorway of Tom's bedroom in amazement, because everywhere on shelves around the walls were all kinds of toy cars and other vehicles.

"Where did you get so many?" he asked as he wandered around the room.

"It's been my hobby for years. Every birthday and Christmas I get more," Tom replied.

Set up on the floor were ramps, roadways and tunnels, and it wasn't long before there were cars whizzing around the room in every direction. Calvin noticed one car still in its box and he asked Tom about it.

"That's my favourite car. I don't use it much because I don't want it bashed about," said Tom. The car was a Porsche, ice-blue coloured, with shiny silver bumpers. It gleamed in the light. Tom hesitated a moment, then gave it to Calvin and said, "You can play with it if you like but don't let it bash into the others."

"Thanks," said Calvin, "I'll be careful." And he was.

The boys carried on zooming the cars around the room, Calvin being extra careful with the ice-blue Porsche. Soon there was a call from downstairs that tea was ready. The boys raced down; it was hungry work playing with the cars. After tea they watched sport on television and then it was time for Calvin to go home.

"He seemed a nice boy," said Tom's mother, after they had said goodbye.

"Yes, I think I'll invite him to my birthday party next month," said Tom, as he settled down in front of the television again.

Suddenly his mum turned the set off. "Upstairs, young man, and tidy your room up."

"I'll do it later."

"Now," said his mother sternly, in a way that meant that there was no arguing.

Tom went upstairs and started to put his cars away. He had almost finished when he noticed the box for his ice-blue Porsche. It was empty. He was puzzled because he did not usually play with the Porsche. Then he remembered that he had let Calvin play with it and a terrible feeling came over him. He began to search frantically but it was nowhere to be seen. Calvin must have taken it. He had stolen it!

Tom has a problem now. What do you think he should do about it?

Tom searched one more time just to be sure. It had definitely gone. He suddenly felt dreadful. Not only had he lost his favourite car but he felt betrayed by his new friend. He then began to feel very angry. How dare Calvin come into his house and steal from him! How dare he accept his kindness and hospitality and then do this! How dare he be so horrible after Tom had gone out of his way to be friendly! Tom suddenly knew what he was going to do.

All weekend Tom thought about what Calvin had done. He kept turning it over in his mind. He was boiling inside but he would get even in the best possible way. He didn't tell his parents about the missing car. They would only say he should look after his things more carefully. There was no point in asking Calvin to give it back, he would just deny it. No, Tom had made up his mind what he was going to do.

Monday morning came and Tom walked purposefully to school. Calvin came running over to him. "Hi, Tom. Want to play football?"

Tom stood still and glowered at him. Through clenched teeth he said, "No, I don't want to play with you ever again!" He walked on, leaving a stunned Calvin behind him.

The bell rang and everyone went into school. Calvin was still sitting next to Tom and throughout the morning he kept glancing at him to see if he would say why he was angry. Calvin was upset; after all, Tom was his first new friend and he now felt very lonely again. The other children sensed there was trouble between the boys and, as Calvin was new, they all sided with Tom.

The day dragged on and when afternoon playtime came the children rushed out. Calvin stood up and looked at Tom to see if he was coming too but Tom pretended to be finishing a piece of work. Calvin went out, dejected, and Mrs Jones left the room without noticing that Tom was still there. Tom quickly went over to Calvin's tray and took out his pencil case. He opened it and there inside was the black and gold fountain pen. He took it out, put the case away and, walking over to his bag, quickly hid the pen in a pocket. He went out into the playground, feeling very smug. Now Calvin would know what it was like to lose something special.

Home time came and Tom saw with some satisfaction that Calvin was talking to Mrs Jones, tears running down his face. He heard her say that she was sure it must be in the classroom somewhere and they would have a good look once everyone was out of the room. Ha, thought Tom, good luck to them!

On the way home he thought about the pen in his bag. It suddenly felt like a great weight around his shoulders. He felt a strong urge to get rid of it, like a criminal getting rid of the evidence. He looked up and down the street: nobody was watching. He took out the pen, stepped to the side of the road and dropped it down a drain. He saw it disappear into the blackness and heard a satisfying 'plop' as it landed in the water. He walked on down the street. Though he no longer had the pen, it still seemed to weigh heavily on him.

As he opened the door, Tom was greeted by his mother. She was just putting the hoover away after her usual Monday clean. "You're getting careless with your things," she said.

"What do you mean?" asked Tom. A shiver went through him: he had a horrible feeling that things were going to collapse around him.

"Look what I found in the corner under your bed."

There, sitting on the kitchen table, was his ice-blue Porsche.

Discussion/Reflection

1. How do you think Tom felt when he saw the car sitting on the table?
2. What good things can you say about Tom?
3. What do you think Calvin felt when Tom ignored him?
4. How do you think Calvin would feel if he learned the truth?
5. Have you ever been in the same situation as Tom? Have you ever blamed someone for something they did not do? Think about what you would do if you were Tom in the story.
6. Think about whether you would have acted differently from Tom.
7. What should Tom do now?

Prayer

Lord, help us to be kind in all we do. Help us to follow the example set by Jesus and to forgive those who do wrong. Amen.

Religious Links

Jesus taught his friends to ask for forgiveness and to be ready to forgive. In his best-known prayer, he said, 'Forgive us our wrongdoings, as we forgive others.' Even when he was being crucified, he prayed to God to forgive the people responsible (Matthew 6:12, Luke 23:34).

Follow-up Activities

1. This story is not quite finished. Children could discuss what Tom should do next, then together decide on (or write) an ending to the story.
2. Both Tom and Calvin show strong feelings in the story. In groups, children could make a list of words describing their feelings then discuss the meanings of these words and the feelings described.

FEELINGS

2
The Lamb

There were many children in Class J who had never been to a farm before. Of course they had seen farms on television and passed them when travelling by car or bus. But they had never walked around a farm, smelled the farm smells or touched the animals. The class had been studying how our food is produced, so Mrs Jones thought that it would be a good idea to visit a farm. Highfield was a mixed farm that grew a variety of crops and also had cows and sheep.

When the children alighted from the coach there were the usual remarks about the smell. Calvin held his nose and said he wouldn't let go until they left but Mrs Jones reminded him that it might be difficult to eat his lunch and breathe at the same time.

The farmer, Mr Marks, greeted the children and told them something about the farm and how it worked. Mrs Jones then split the class into groups and, while one group was taken into the milking parlour, the rest were asked to sketch some of the farm machinery and implements. Once they had all been to see how the cows were milked, it was time to feed the lambs. This was the highlight of the morning.

Mr Marks had several lambs that needed to be bottle-fed, so he gave a couple of bottles to each group, lined the children along a wall, and with a grin, warned them to watch out. The children stood there not knowing what to expect as he disappeared round the corner. They heard the barn door opened and then the frenzied patter of hooves. Seven lambs came hurtling round the corner and raced to the children. They ravenously attacked the bottles and there was instant pandemonium, with squeals of delight from the children and milk spraying everywhere. The adults watching fell about with laughter as children and lambs became covered with milk. It was over all too quickly and the lambs were herded into a pen nearby.

By now it was lunchtime, so after washing their hands the children tucked into their own food of sandwiches and crisps. They ate quickly as they sat on the grass near the lamb pen and then ran over to stroke the lambs. Lakshmi, Tom and Lisa were particularly taken with a little black-faced lamb who kept trying to suck their fingers.

Soon Mrs Jones was calling the children together to get ready for the afternoon session. She asked them first to make sure that no litter from their lunch was left on the ground. The children hurriedly packed their bags as Mr Marks joined them and they began their walk along the outlying fields to see the range of crops grown at Highfield.

As they walked away, some of the children called goodbye to the seven lambs who were pressing against the fence watching them. Nobody saw the empty crisp packet lying beside a tree stump. Before long, a little gust of wind picked it up and trundled it along the ground. It twisted and twirled first one way then another, gradually moving nearer to the lambs' enclosure.

How did the crisp packet get there?
What do you think is going to happen to it?

The children were beginning to get bored with looking at fields of wheat and potatoes. It wasn't as exciting as seeing the animals. They began to walk back to the farm buildings. Lakshmi asked Mr Marks if they could feed the lambs again. He explained that they weren't due for their next feed until later in the day but he said the children could spend a few minutes stroking them before leaving.

As they approached the farm buildings some of the children raced over to the lamb enclosure. The lambs were at the opposite end but as soon as they saw the children they trotted over to see if there was any food to be had. That is to say, six came over but one was left lying on the ground. It had a little black face and it wasn't moving.

Tom and Lakshmi began to stroke the excited lambs but they stopped suddenly when Lisa cried out, "Look, something's wrong with that lamb!" Other children ran over and started to point and shout to Mrs Jones and Mr Marks. The farmer told the children to stand back as he quickly climbed into the enclosure and ran to the stricken lamb. He began to examine the lamb to see what was wrong with it. He felt its body to find a pulse, to see if it was still alive.

He said he could feel a faint pulse but it was fading fast. He suggested to Mrs Jones that perhaps she should take the children back to the bus right away but nobody really wanted to move. The children were stunned into silence, one or two biting their bottom lips.

Mr Marks felt helpless, he didn't know what was wrong. Then he thought of something and began to feel inside the lamb's mouth. The children watched as he slowly pulled something out. Within seconds the lamb gave a huge snort and began to struggle to its feet. The children all gave a large sigh of relief and began to smile again.

Mr Marks walked over to the children, frowning. "I found this lodged down the lamb's throat. It nearly choked to death."
He held up an empty crisp packet. The children stopped smiling.

Discussion/Reflection
1. Why did the children stop smiling when Mr Marks held up the crisp packet? Why was he frowning? What was he feeling at that moment?
2. How did the children feel at the end of the story?
3. How would you have felt if you had been at the farm and had seen the lamb nearly dying?
4. How do you feel when you see people dropping litter? What do you think you could do to prevent it?

Prayer
Lord, from the lowly ant to the mighty elephant, all are your creatures. So are we. Help us to care for them all. Amen.

Religious Links
Many religions have stories about respect for all life. Jews and Christians have a Creation story in Genesis 1, in which people are told to look after the world, including its plants and animals. Other religions have Creation stories as well, such as the Hindu story of Vishnu and Brahma. Psalm 104:16–26 looks at wildlife in a very poetic way.

Follow-up Activities
1. Discuss the litter problem in your own area. What are dangers of leaving litter? What should we do with our litter?
2. Design anti-litter posters.
3. Study the Country Code. In groups, children could prepare a drama presentation showing what may happen when we do not follow the Country Code.

FEELINGS

3
The Long Wait

"What time is it?" shouted Subatra.

"It's five minutes after the last time you asked," called her mother from the kitchen. "There's a clock in the lounge – use it!"

Subatra was looking out of the window, watching intently down the road. She was excited because she had been invited out by her new classmate, Joanne. And most important, this was the first time she was going out without her sister, Lakshmi. They always did everything together because they were twins. But recently their differences had begun to show. Subatra enjoyed sporting activities, while Lakshmi preferred to read or play chess on her computer. Also, Subatra was far more impatient and excitable, always acting first and thinking later.

A few days ago, Joanne had asked Subatra to go swimming with her. It was agreed that Joanne would call for Subatra at two o'clock. It was now five minutes to two and Subatra was getting very eager. She enjoyed swimming and this was a chance to get to know Joanne a little better.

"Is it two o'clock yet?" called Subatra to her mother again.

Her mother walked into the room, saying, "Look, she'll be here any minute. Why don't you wait at the gate, then you'll be able to see her coming?"

Subatra grabbed her swimming bag and went to the front door.

Lakshmi called out from her room, "Have a good time!" but Subatra was out of the door and down the path without hearing her. She was picturing in her mind being at the swimming pool, diving in and swimming strong strokes down the centre of the pool. She knew that Joanne was a good swimmer and she was desperate to show Joanne how well she could swim.

She kept looking down the road but there was no sign of Joanne. "Where is she?" she kept saying to herself. She ran into the house and looked at the clock – ten past two. Joanne was now ten minutes late.

"Are you back already?" asked her mother.

"She hasn't arrived yet, she's late," snapped Subatra.

"Don't you get bad-tempered with me, young lady. It's not my fault your friend's late," replied her mother.

Subatra walked to the gate again and continued to wait. By half past two, she was very agitated and angry. She was so looking forward to going swimming and now she was beginning to feel really let down.

She walked back into the house and stomped upstairs to her bedroom, muttering angrily about never being friends with Joanne again.

Subatra is really getting into a stew about being let down. Instead of getting angry about the situation, what should she do?
What do you think of Joanne's role in this?

The next day was Sunday and Subatra sulked around the house all day.

"Why don't you telephone your friend and find out what happened?" suggested her mother.

"No, it's up to her to phone me," retorted Subatra.

All day she was working out in her mind what she was going to say to Joanne. She would say something really cutting, loudly in front of her friends so that they would know how unreliable Joanne was. Even that night she was restless, her thoughts spinning round the coming confrontation with Joanne.

On Monday morning Subatra arrived at school early. She wanted to be there before Joanne. Slowly the playground filled up and Subatra looked for Joanne, ready to confront her. She had told a few of her friends what she was going to do and they stood around with her, waiting to see what would happen. But when the bell went Joanne had not appeared. Subatra felt a great sense of frustration; she really wanted to get this unpleasantness over with. How dare Joanne do this to her!

The children sat down and Mrs Jones began to call the register. She was half-way through when Mr Hall came in and began to speak to her. His voice was quiet and serious but just loud enough for the children sitting nearby to hear. Subatra was among them and what she heard made her feel dreadful inside.

"I'm afraid Joanne won't be at school today. Her grandfather died suddenly on Saturday morning and the family have all gone to stay with her grandmother. She should be back by the end of the week."

Discussion/Reflection
1. How do you think Subatra feels now? Does she still feel angry?
2. What should she do next?
3. Can Joanne be blamed for what happened?
4. What is meant by 'acting first and thinking later'?
5. Has anyone ever let you down? Was there a good reason? How did you feel about it?
6. Have you ever let a friend down? Think about how you could avoid letting someone down.

Prayer
Let us pray that we can control our anger and try to understand why people behave the way they do. Lord, help us to be patient and understanding.

Religious Links
In the Letter of James, 3:5-6, it says: 'The tongue – it is a small member but it can make huge claims. What an immense stack of timber can be set ablaze by the tiniest spark! And the tongue is in effect a fire.' It can cause massive damage.

Christians believe that the Holy Spirit is like a good tongue. It will give them the right things to say and create great goodness. (Acts 2, Mark 13:11).

Follow-up Activities
1. Three lines of discussion could be taken: looking at anger; making wrong assumptions about people; and relying on someone and then being let down.
2. Subatra began to tell others about how Joanne had let her down. Spreading untruths about someone could be explored in the form of drama.

4
The Concert

THEME: respect for other people's talents

Tom slipped the ball through the defence to Calvin and ran on to receive the return ball. But Calvin overhit the pass and the ball spun off the playground towards a group of children watching.

"Give us the ball, Brainbox," called Tom to a short, blond-haired boy. Philip, alias Brainbox, picked up the ball and threw it towards the footballers. He didn't dare kick it, because with his two left feet it would probably end up in the swimming pool. Without thanking him, the boys carried on playing while Philip longingly looked on.

It wasn't that Philip longed to be a good footballer, it was just that his greatest wish was to be part of the 'in' crowd. He desperately wanted to be liked by the other boys, especially Tom and Calvin, everyone's favourites. The trouble was that he didn't have a sporting bone in his body. He swam like a brick, he always came last at sports day, he would hit his own wicket when at bat in cricket and he was always out at first post in rounders. He hated times when teams were being chosen by the two captains because he was always the last one to be picked.

Philip's only claim to popularity was his nickname, Brainbox. This was because his real hobby was reading and as a consequence he was very knowledgeable. He could always be relied upon to answer questions correctly. One day Tom had made the remark, "Leave it to old Brainbox, he'll get it right", and the nickname stuck. At first Philip didn't like it and once he deliberately gave a wrong answer. The trouble was that everyone was so surprised that they laughed at him which made him feel much worse than being called Brainbox.

When the whistle blew for the end of play the children hurried inside. There would be no Maths today; instead, they were having the first main practice for the end of term concert. This year they were going to perform *Joseph and his Amazing Technicolor Dreamcoat*. The main character of Joseph was to be played by Calvin because of his excellent singing voice. Tom's good Elvis impersonation had gained him the part of Pharaoh. Philip wanted to be one of the brothers but he was made a guard because he was good at standing still.

Over the next few weeks the rehearsals went well. The children had learned their words and scripts were no longer needed. Mr Bell, the music teacher, said that the singing was the best yet. Both children and teachers were looking forward to the performance evening, when disaster struck.

In assembly one morning Mr Hall, the Headteacher, told them, "I'm afraid I have some bad news for you. Mr Bell has been in a car accident. He is not seriously hurt but he has broken his arm. Unfortunately that means we have no pianist for the concert. Unless one of your parents can help, we shall just have to postpone it."

Oh no! The whole school was silent. They could not believe the bad news.

An arm went up. "Couldn't he play with one hand?" asked someone.

"No, the music is much too complicated for that," replied Mr Hall.

They were all very disappointed. They had already designed the programme. Tickets were on sale. Tom's grandmother was going to make a special trip to see him. Calvin's mother had made the coloured coat. All that time and effort wasted: surely there was someone else who could play the piano?

"Yes, Philip, do you know someone who can play?" said Mr Hall to Philip, who had put his hand up.

"Yes, sir, I do," he replied. Everyone looked at him.

"One of your parents, is it?" asked Mr Hall.

"No, sir. I can play the piano," said Philip. There was an immediate buzz around the room and the nudging of elbows. Philip continued, "And some of the recorders are very good, and Lisa and Joanne could play their clarinets."

"I don't know, it's very difficult," said Mr Hall, looking at Philip and the other children he had named, who were now beginning to look excited at the idea.

"Could we take the music home over the weekend and practise? Then you could decide on Monday if we are good enough," suggested Philip.

Mr Hall agreed to this. As soon as assembly was over, Philip got the group of five recorder players and two clarinettists together and arranged to meet at his house on Saturday afternoon.

On the way home Tom approached Philip and said, "Are you sure you can play?"

"Of course, I've been having lessons for years," said Philip.

"So has my sister but she can still only play 'Three Blind Mice' with two fingers. I hope you're right, otherwise everyone's going to be disappointed," warned Tom.

I hope I'm right as well, thought Philip, beginning to wonder what he had got himself into.

Philip is putting a lot of pressure on himself.
Why do you think he is doing this?

Monday morning came. Philip was deep in thought as he walked to school. Tom and Calvin went over to him when he entered the playground. "We hope your piano playing is better than your football," laughed Tom.

"How did your practice go, Brainbox?" asked Calvin who showed more concern about the situation than Tom did.

"Not too bad," replied Philip. "We only had time to practise a few songs. If Mr Hall thinks it's all right then we'll stay in at lunchtimes and practise the others."

"I can't wait to hear this," chuckled Tom as he wandered off.

"Don't worry about him," said Calvin. "I'm sure you'll do your best." Though Calvin was trying to be kind, it was obvious to Philip by the way he spoke that he wasn't too hopeful about their ability to play the music.

During the lunch break Philip and his group practised in one of the classrooms furthest away from the playground. Nobody was allowed to listen. Next it was time for the afternoon rehearsal and all the cast went into the hall. Tom was muttering about it being a waste of time when Mr Hall called for silence.

"Well, children, we'll start off with your favourite song, 'Any Dream Will Do'. Right, Philip, over to you."

The hall was hushed as Philip sat at the piano. He began to play the introduction but when he reached the verse no one sang! They were so amazed at his beautiful playing that they forgot to sing. Philip stopped and looked round, then at a nod from Mr Hall he began again. This time the children did sing and, when the recorders and clarinets came in during the other verses, they sang with real feeling. At the end of the song they all clapped spontaneously and Philip could hear Tom shouting, "Well done, Brainbox!"

"Well, everyone," said Mr Hall. "I think we have a concert again!" They all cheered.

The run-up to the concert went smoothly. Mr Bell was able to come in and help Philip and the other musicians. The concert itself was an enormous success: many parents said it was the best they had ever seen.

The children began to look upon Philip now with more respect. This didn't mean that Tom and his friends allowed him to play football with them but he was asked to hold their coats for them while they played. When he handed back their coats at whistle time they simply said, "Thanks, Phil." It wasn't much but it was enough for him.

Discussion/Reflection

1. Why do you think Philip was pleased when the other boys said, "Thanks, Phil"?
2. At the beginning of the story, why was Philip not accepted by the other boys? How do you think he felt?
3. What was Tom's reaction when Philip offered to play the piano?
4. Who showed more kindness, Tom or Calvin?
5. Do you know what your friends are good at? If not, maybe you should talk to them about it.
6. How do you feel when someone says 'Well done' to you? Does it make you feel good inside? When was the last time *you* praised someone?

Prayer

Let us ask God to help us to discover our skills and use them in the best possible way. Lord, help us to use wisely the gifts we have been given.

Religious Links

Paul suggests that Christians are like a body with different parts, each of the parts needs all the others, and has to be willing to give of its best to the others and to receive from them what they have to give. (1 Corinthians 12:12–26)

Follow-up Activities

1. Children could discuss the various ways in which courage can be shown. They could begin by looking at how Philip showed courage.
2. Try to discover a hidden talent of each member of the class. Some children could prepare a short talk about their talent or about someone else's.
3. Children could look at words and gestures that show praise and the kinds of feelings they generate.

5
What's Wrong with Marie?

THEME: being jealous of a younger brother

The knock on Mr Hall's door was very insistent.

"Come in," he called. He looked up from his writing to see Calvin and Tom in the doorway. "Yes, boys, what can I do for you?"

"We've come to tell you there's something going on in the girls' toilets," said Tom.

Mr Hall looked suspiciously at the two boys. "Have you been chasing some of the girls?"

"No, sir," said Calvin defensively." We were just passing and we could hear crying in there."

"OK. Sorry, boys. I'll go and see what's happening," said Mr Hall, putting down his pen as he realized it would be a waste of time trying to do any work this lunchtime.

The first thing he had to do was to disperse the small crowd starting to gather around the door of the girls' toilet. Once that was accomplished he was able to give his attention to Marie, who was leaning her head against the wall, sobbing her heart out. Mr Hall realized that this was no larking about, she was in real distress.

"Come on, Marie, tell me what the problem is."

Marie did not answer. In fact she was crying so much she couldn't say anything.

"Let's go and find a quiet place to sit down," said Mr Hall, as he led her out.

Some of Marie's friends who were worried about her came up to them but Mr Hall shooed them away.

He led Marie to his office and sat her down on a large easy chair. "Now, tell me what the problem is," he said.

Marie just looked down, dabbing her eyes with the tissue he gave her. She said nothing.

Mr Hall was a little puzzled by this. Marie was one of the more sensible, mature children in Mrs Jones's class; this was quite out of character for her. He tried to question her further.

"Are you feeling unwell in any way?" No answer.

"Have some of the other children been horrible to you?" No answer. He had felt sure that this was probably the case but there was no reaction at all to that question.

"Are you having problems with your work?" No answer.

"Is everything all right at home?" No answer but Marie reacted by burying her face in her hands. Mr Hall realized that something serious was upsetting Marie and it would take a while before he could find out. The whistle blew for the end of lunch break.

"You don't really want to go into class at the moment, do you?" he asked her. Marie shook her head.

"I'll be back in a moment. You just rest and calm yourself." He went to Marie's classroom where Mrs Jones was just about to call the register. He asked the class if anyone knew why Marie was so upset but no one did. Mrs Jones suggested that maybe a close relative or perhaps a pet had recently died but again no one knew, not even Marie's closest friends. All the class were genuinely concerned. What was wrong with Marie?

Mr Hall went to the infant class. Marie's younger brother, Matthew, had just started school that term. However, Matthew had not come to school that morning and there had been no message to explain why.

The Head decided to telephone Marie's parents. The phone rang for a long time, then, just as he was going to ring off, Marie's mother answered. She had just that minute returned from taking Matthew to the hospital. Apparently he had fallen on to a glass-topped table, broken the glass and cut his hand. Though they were all shocked because of the blood everywhere, Matthew's cut would heal and there would be no permanent damage to his hand. They both agreed that this was probably why Marie was upset and it would be best for her to go home. She would soon cheer up once she saw that Matthew was all right.

Mr Hall went back to his office to tell Marie the good news. When he had finished he said, "We both think it would be a good idea for you to go home, so if you want to get all your things together I'll take you now."

But he didn't get the reaction he was expecting. Marie looked up at him, tears still in her eyes as she said, "I can't go home."

"Why, what's the problem? Don't you want to see that your brother is all right after his accident?"

There was a pause and then Marie said, "But it wasn't an accident."

"What do you mean? Your mother said it was an accident."

"She doesn't know what really happened."

Then Marie began to tell her story.

It began during Maths the previous day. Tom and Calvin were rushing around the room and accidentally knocked her calculator on to the floor. When she needed it for her work it wouldn't come on. Philip allowed her to use his but the buttons were so small that she kept getting the sums wrong. By the end of the lesson she had only half finished so Mrs Jones said she had to finish the work at home. That was all right because she could borrow her father's calculator.

At the end of the day she collected Matthew from the infant class and walked home. Their mother had milk-shakes and biscuits ready for them on the kitchen table. Then further disaster struck. When Matthew reached across the table for his own drink he knocked Marie's glass over. Not only was there milk-shake all over the table but also over her Maths books! Marie shrieked out, Matthew cried and her mother told Marie not to be so silly, it was only an accident. Marie pointed out that her books were wet but her mother said that her books should not have been there in the first place.

That evening Marie started to work on her Maths, using a rather soggy book. The work was going well until she came to a problem she didn't really understand. Her father had gone out to a meeting. Her mother was helping Matthew with his reading book but she said she would be along to help her in a few minutes. After another hour Marie was getting more frustrated with her Maths. She went to look for her mother again and found her making the next day's packed lunch. Her mother said she was sorry, she had forgotten: after reading with Matthew she been busy sorting out the washing. It was getting late, so she suggested that Marie asked Dad to help her in the morning. Marie wasn't too sure about this because it was always a rush in the morning but there was no point in arguing.

Marie didn't sleep well because she was worrying about her Maths, so she got up feeling grumpy. When she came down to breakfast, her father was reading a story Matthew had written. She remarked that it was a load of rubbish. At this her father glowered at her and told her not to be in such a bad mood. When she asked him for help with her Maths he said he was not going to help anyone who was so rude.

Tears of anger welled up in her eyes. Matthew had gone to play with his cars in the sitting room. She watched him playing happily and decided that he was the cause of all her problems. He spilt milk-shake all over her books, he managed to get help with his reading and had his work read out. At that moment, their mother called out for them to put their coats on. As Matthew ran by, Marie stuck out her foot to trip him up. But instead of falling on to the carpet he flew through the air and landed on the glass coffee table. With a loud scream he crashed through the glass table-top. Marie stood there, shocked at what she had done. Her parents came rushing in. Her mother comforted her while her father wrapped Matthew's arm in a cloth and got him into the car to take him to hospital. Her mother went to the hospital as well and Marie came to school.

"So you see," finished Marie, "it was all my fault. They think it was an accident but it wasn't."

"What made you do it?" asked Mr Hall.

"I don't know. It just seemed so unfair. Matthew was getting all the attention and he ruined my books."

"But that was an accident," said Mr Hall." It's very difficult for parents to give all their children equal time and run a household as well. Don't forget you had all their attention before he was born. What are you going to do?"

"I don't know," replied Marie.

"Well, I told your mother I'd bring you home now, so you've got the car ride home to decide."

They were both quiet in the car; there didn't seem to be anything more to say. When they got to Marie's house she got out of the car and said, "Thank you for bringing me home."

Mr Hall looked at her and simply said, "Good luck." He watched her go up the path to the front door. She had stopped crying and seemed calmer now. She appeared to walk with a purpose. Somehow he knew what she was going to say to her parents.

Discussion/Reflection

1. What do you think Marie was going to say to her parents?
2. What were her feelings before the accident and then after the accident?
3. Do you think it was fair to blame Matthew?
4. At what stage do you think she should have acted differently?
5. How will Marie's parents feel when they hear the truth? How do you think they should react?
6. Think about the things that make you feel jealous. How do you control these feelings?
7. Have you ever reacted badly, like Marie, and regretted it later? Did you try to make things right in the end?
8. Is it always harder for older sisters and brothers than younger ones? Why or why not?

Prayer

Let us pray for God's help to enable us to be fair, just, honest and forgiving to those who wrong us. Amen.

Religious Links

Jealous resentment occurs in the stories Jacob and Esau (Genesis 27:1–46) and Sarah and Ishmael (Genesis 21:9–13) but God didn't approve. In 1 Samuel 18:6–16, Saul's resentful jealousy of David led to attempted murder.

Follow-up Activities

1. Discuss with the children times when they feel jealous. Talk about their feelings and how they could control them.
2. Two other emotions arising from this story are feeling 'sorry' and forgiving others. Discussions about these feelings could lead to writing or drama.

FEELINGS

6
The Quiz

> **THEME: cheating**

When Tom got to school he had a funny feeling that there was something he should have done. He had spent the weekend watching sport on television and now he wished he'd telephoned Calvin to find out what they had to do. The problem was that the piece of paper he'd written the details on was left in his trouser pocket when his mother put his clothes into the washing machine on Friday evening. All he ended up with was a soggy lump of paper. At the time he felt that that would be a good enough excuse not to bother; now he felt differently.

Calvin was already in the playground when he arrived. "Ready for the test then?" he asked.

Tom looked puzzled. "What test?" he asked. —

Calvin grinned at him and realized that for once he was going to be one up on Tom. Though they were the best of friends, they were also very competitive, each trying to do better than the other. "You know, the test on all the topics we have covered this term. Mrs Jones told us about it on Friday."

Tom suddenly remembered. There was to be a test on the topics they had been working on recently. There were also going to be some general knowledge questions. Now he realized what it was he should have done. He had not listened carefully enough. He remembered Mrs Jones saying something about general knowledge but not about the rest. When his bit of paper was destroyed in the washing machine he decided you couldn't study for a general knowledge test anyway, so he didn't bother. Now he was worried.

"When do you think we'll have the test?" asked Tom.

"I'm sure it'll be as soon as we get in," said Calvin.

In fact, the test was going to be after playtime. So, when playtime came, Tom asked Mrs Jones if he could stay in to, as he put it, finish off his studying but she said no. He wished he'd said that he felt unwell – usually that would have worked.

After play the children were told to clear their tables except for a pencil and rubber. Mrs Jones moved children around so that no one would be tempted to cheat, but there were more children than spare places. Tom found himself sitting next to Philip, the brightest boy in the class. Mrs Jones gave out the papers and said, "When I say

'begin' you are to turn over the paper and write your name on the top, and then you can start. Begin."

Tom turned over the paper, wrote his name at the top and began to read. As he looked at the first few questions he realized just how unprepared he was. He couldn't answer them at all. A feeling of panic came over him. In his mind he could imagine seeing his score, the lowest in the class. What would his parents think?

He looked at Philip busily writing away. He noticed that his paper was facing him because Philip was left-handed. Philip must have sensed Tom's eyes because he looked up. He saw the panicked look in Tom's face and he carefully moved his arm so that Tom could see his answers. Tom looked around to make sure that Mrs Jones wasn't looking, then began to copy from Philip's paper. He didn't dare do this when Mrs Jones was nearby, so then he tried to make up the answers as best he could. Anyway that would probably be better, he thought, because it would look suspicious if he and Philip handed in two identical tests.

Afterwards, Tom managed to whisper his thanks to Philip while they put their things away in readiness for lunch.

"What did you think of the test?" asked Calvin at the dinner table.

"It wasn't too difficult at all," said Tom, grinning to Philip. Calvin looked at the two of them, wondering what the joke was. He was a bit surprised at Tom's reaction, knowing that he hadn't studied, and a tiny suspicion began to creep into his mind but he didn't say anything.

On Friday afternoon there was a buzz of excitement in the classroom because Mrs Jones was going to give out the results of the test. She handed back the marked papers and Tom felt a wave of relief when he saw that he got 38 out of 50. Philip got 45, the top mark, as expected.

"What did you get, Calvin?" Tom asked.

"Not as much as I hoped, only 32," was the reply.

When Tom told him his own score Calvin could not believe it but before he could say anything Mrs Jones made an announcement.

"Class, may I have your attention. Mr Hall has asked me to pick a team for the inter-school quiz competition next week. I thought that the best way to do this would be to choose the top four children from the test I have just marked. So, the team will be Philip, who will be team captain, Joanne, Marie and Tom, with Calvin as substitute."

Tom was alarmed. He knew he wasn't good enough to be in the team but what could he say? To back out now would mean admitting he cheated in the test.

What do you think Tom should do?
Was Philip wrong in letting Tom cheat?

Mrs Jones went on, "Next week I would like to see the team and you as well, Calvin, so that we can practise the type of questions you might get."

Afterwards Calvin went up to Tom and said, "Did you really do that test on your own?"

Tom was about to answer, when Philip walked up to them and said, "Do you want any help over the weekend? I could bring over some of my general knowledge books."

Calvin looked at both of them and said, "You're just a cheat, you shouldn't be in the team." And he walked off. He felt it was all very unfair.

Over the weekend Philip tried to coach Tom but Tom's heart was not in the work. He wanted to be out playing football, instead of studying. The more Philip tried, the more it seemed that Tom just couldn't get the right answers. It wasn't that Tom was not very bright; it was just that he liked to think things through at his own pace. In a quiz you had to be very quick and that wasn't the way he worked.

The first practice session came too quickly for Tom. The five of them sat facing Mrs Jones. "Are you ready?" she asked. "The first to put their hand up can answer the question. What does H_2O represent?"

Four hands went up, but not Tom's. His mind went blank.

"Water," said Marie.

"Correct. What is the difference between deciduous and coniferous trees?"

Again four hands went up right away and, by the time Tom managed to think of an answer, Joanne had already started. And so it went on, the other four being noticeably quicker than Tom. When they had finished Mrs Jones asked Tom to stay behind.

"Are you all right, Tom? You didn't seem to be on the ball today." she said.

Tom felt that this was his chance to put things straight but all he managed to say was, "I don't feel very well, Miss."

For the next few days Tom didn't come to school. Apparently he had a bug of some sort. Then the day of the quiz came. Calvin had been told that if Tom was not well enough then he would be in the team. But his heart sank when he saw Tom, with his mother, coming into school. Through the classroom window, Calvin could see them talking. Tom didn't look very happy and Calvin wondered what was going on.

When the children went into the classroom, Tom was already at his desk. Mrs Jones announced that all the class would be able to watch the quiz. She finished by saying, "Calvin, Tom doesn't feel up to taking part today, so you can take his place." Looking straight at Tom, she said, "I'm sure you'll do just as well."

Discussion/Reflection
1. What do you think Tom and his mother discussed with Mrs Jones?
2. Why do you think Mrs Jones didn't give a full reason for Tom withdrawing?
3. How do you think Tom felt when Calvin called him a cheat? What were Calvin's feelings?
4. At what point could Tom have sorted out the situation?
5. Do you think Philip should have let Tom copy from him?
6. Can Calvin trust Tom again? Can they still be close friends?

Prayer
The Gospel of John talks about *doing* the truth. Let us be silent for a moment or two to remember in God's presence that the truth is not just what we say but what we do as well.

Religious Links
Are we on the side of truth? The great world religions teach that who- ever belongs to the truth listens to God (John 18:37).

Follow-up Activities
1. The concept of cheating in sport is often in the news. Children can discuss why people cheat and what can be done about it.
2. Copying work or answers in a test is another form of cheating. Discuss as a class who suffers most when this happens. What are the long-term problems?

FEELINGS

7
The School Rule

THEME: the importance of rules

The children filed out class by class after assembly. Mr Hall, the Headteacher, had been talking about the importance of rules. He reminded them about some of the school rules, in particular the one about no running in school. Little did he realize how soon that rule was going to be broken and in what a smashing style.

It all happened at playtime that morning. Mrs Jones usually allowed the children to take two balls outside to play with – one for football and one for netball. Boys and girls were allowed to play both games but two children were responsible for collecting and returning the balls.

At playtime Calvin collected the one for football but nobody collected the one for netball. Outside, the children gathered around, looking at one another.

"Well, who's got the ball?" asked Subatra.

"Joanne is responsible for bringing it out but she's away today," said Philip. "Shall I go in and get it?"

"No, I'll get it," said Subatra. She thought it would be a good chance to be a team organizer in place of Joanne. Subatra was quite a bossy girl who liked to have things done her way.

"Well, hurry up or the whistle will go before we even start," urged Marie.

Subatra raced off. She stopped at the entrance door, checked that there was no one about and ran down the corridor to the classroom. She found the ball in its usual place. Checking to make sure that the coast was clear, she dashed out of the door and began running down the corridor past the other classrooms. Just at the wrong moment Mr Bell came out of his room, carrying an overhead projector. Subatra crashed into him. The projector shot one way and she another. There was a loud smashing sound as the overhead projector hit the wall and fell to the floor. Subatra also fell, feeling a sharp pain across her forehead. Mr Bell stood there, wondering what had hit him and looking at his empty arms where the projector had been. After a few seconds all that could be heard was the ball rolling down the corridor.

Mr Hall and Mrs Jones came running to see what was the matter: they must have heard the crash from the staffroom. Subatra began to feel something running down her face. She put her hand to her forehead and looked with horror at the blood on her fingers.

"Come on, let's have a look at you," said Mrs Jones gently to Subatra.

"What happened?" asked Mr Hall.

"I was coming out of my classroom when this youngster came running down the corridor. I was carrying the overhead projector and I think she must have cut herself on the broken glass," explained Mr Bell.

While Mrs Jones took Subatra to the office for some first aid, the other two teachers picked up the broken overhead projector and the bits of broken glass.

Subatra was in a state of shock, especially after seeing her own blood. She felt very shaky and sick. Mrs Jones wiped the blood from her face and carefully put a bandage over the cut.

"I think you should go to the hospital. Is there anybody at home?" asked Mrs Jones. Subatra nodded and Mrs Jones telephoned. Mrs Chatterji quickly came round to the school and Mr Hall drove them both to the local casualty department.

Subatra was lucky. She had a cut which needed a few stitches but otherwise she was all right. The overhead projector was a write-off and the school had to spend £400 on another one. A few days later in assembly Mr Hall once again spoke about the rule that there was to be no running in school and this time the children really listened. Several faces turned towards Subatra who, with her bandaged head, went hot with embarrassment.

Discussion/Reflection
1. Why do you think Subatra was embarrassed?
2. How do you think Subatra felt when she realized what she had done?
3. Why do we have a rule about no running in the school?
4. How would you feel if we had a world without rules?

Prayer
Rules make us safe and secure. Let us give thanks to God for rules that protect us from thoughtless people and rules that protect us from our own thoughtlessness.

Religious Links
In the Jewish religion, the Ten Commandments (Deuteronomy 5) are obvious rules to look at. In Matthew 22: 36-39, Jesus, as a practising Jew, is asked which are the most important. He replies that all laws are based on the first two – to love God and to love your neighbour as you would love yourself.

In Islam, the Qur'an sets out how Muslims should live their lives. They believe that, without this instruction from Allah, people may turn to evil. Muslims believe that Allah has given everyone the choice to do either right or wrong. Ask the children about times when they have had a choice such as this.

The Buddha gave his followers rules to help them live contented lives. These include instructions to live simply and to meditate.

Follow-up Activities
1. Discuss the school and/or classroom rules and why they are needed.
2. Children could agree in pairs or small groups on class rules they would like to have. Together the groups could draw up a list of class rules.
3. Children could investigate other rules outside the school, e.g. the Highway Code, and find out how laws are made.

8
The Mountain Bike

Calvin and Tom looked at the row of mountain bikes in the shop. The fluorescent colours of the stripes and patterns made the bikes look dazzling. The boys wandered along the row, touching the handlebars, stroking the knobbly tyres and clutching at the brakes. Suddenly Tom dashed over to a bright yellow machine and said, "This is the same as mine."

"Did your parents really pay £250?" asked Calvin.

"Well, it was a sort of combined Christmas and birthday present," replied Tom. Tom did not think it unusual to be given expensive presents. He always got what he wanted, especially if he told his parents that all the other boys had one as well.

Calvin looked enviously at the bicycle. He had a birthday coming up soon and his mother asked him that morning what he wanted. He was the only one in his group not to have a bicycle, so that was what he really wanted.

"Can I help you?" asked a sales assistant. He was a tall young man in grey overalls. His tone of voice suggested that he had just spent the morning polishing the bicycles and didn't want grubby little fingers all over them.

"Have you got a brochure about these types of bikes?" asked Calvin.

"If you would like to come this way, I'll see what I can find," he replied coldly. The boys followed him over to the counter where he handed them a glossy brochure. "You'll find a separate price list inside."

Calvin eagerly looked at the pictures as they walked out of the shop. First he liked the red one with twelve gears, then he liked even better the blue one with fifteen gears, but finally he spotted the one he really wanted – a green machine with eighteen gears.

At home he had to wait, rather impatiently, for his mother to return from work. She was a day nurse at the local home for the elderly. Calvin and his mother lived alone in a comfortable little two-bedroomed terraced house. He wished they lived nearer to the school, where Tom lived, but his mother said that it was too expensive in that area. Still, with his new bicycle he wouldn't have to do the long walk any more.

"I'm home," his mother called out as she came through the front door.

"I've decided what I want for my birthday," said Calvin, waving the brochure as he raced to the door.

"Let's have dinner first, then we can sit all evening looking at what you've decided," replied his mother in a rather tired voice.

That evening he showed his mother the brochure. She was quiet as he described the merits of the different bicycles. Then she looked at the price list and slowly shook her head. "I'm sorry, love, I just haven't got the money to pay for any of these. I could probably go to £30 but that really is the limit."

The disappointment was so great that it hurt. Calvin looked away. With tears in his eyes, he ran out of the room, gripping the brochure.

"Oh, Calvin, please understand, the cost of a bicycle is a whole month's wages," called his mother. She decided to leave him be for a while; he would just have to live with his disappointment.

We sometimes have to live with lower expectations.
How should Calvin react to his mother?

The next day was Saturday. Calvin got up late and found his mother busy doing the cleaning. She was lovingly polishing the small grandfather clock sitting in the corner of the lounge. It was a very old clock passed down to them by his grandparents. His mother always looked after it and it was a ritual with her to start on Saturday morning by polishing the clock and then winding it up.

She tried to cheer Calvin up. "How about having your favourite fish and chips today?"

"I don't mind," said Calvin with a shrug.

Nothing more was said about the bicycle during the next few weeks leading up to Calvin's birthday. He didn't offer an alternative idea for a present, in the hope thay his mother might surprise him. He still made out to Tom and the other boys that he was going to get a bicycle. Right up to the very eve of his birthday he lived in hope . After all, his mother had stopped asking him for other ideas so she must have made up her mind.

When Calvin woke up on his birthday morning he looked around his room and there, by his bed , was a box. With great disappointment he picked it up, thinking she had bought him another football. But it was too light for that. Curiosity took over and eagerly he unwrapped the box, then his heart leapt, for it was a cycling helmet! She wouldn't have bought that without a bike as well! Calvin jumped out of bed and raced down the stairs. There, standing in the lounge, was a bicycle. He stood open-mouthed, staring at it. It wasn't a mountain bike. It wasn't green. It wasn't even new. It was a second-hand, brown, drop-handled racing bike.

His mother came up behind him and said, "I knew nothing else would do except a bicycle. I asked the man at the shop if he had a good second-hand one and he recommended this. It's got ten gears, you know. Happy birthday, love." She gave him a kiss and then went off to get breakfast ready.

Calvin didn't know what to say. All the other boys had mountain bikes; he would be the only one with something different. He was supposed to meet the other boys at the recreation ground that afternoon. How could he face his friends with that? Tears welled up in his eyes; the feeling of disappointment and frustration was enormous. What should he do? He told his friends he was getting a bicycle. Which was worse – turning up at the rec with this bike or with no bike at all? He looked at the racing bicycle more closely. It was in very good condition. He sat on the seat, it didn't feel too bad. He decided to cycle to the rec.

That afternoon Calvin whizzed along the road. Tom, Philip and Robert were already at the rec when he got there.

"Is that your new bike?" asked Tom.

"Yes, it's not really what I wanted but it goes well," replied Calvin. He didn't want to say it was all his mum could afford.

"I used to have one like that," said Philip, "before I got my mountain bike." That was the kind of comment Calvin didn't want to hear. But there was worse to come from Robert who was often nasty to the others.

"That kind of bike's rubbish. This bike," he said, patting his gleaming silver mountain bike, "is the best you can get. You can go anywhere on this."

"So you can on this," retorted Calvin.

"What, on an old droopy bars like that?" taunted Robert.

"Come on, let's go round the field," shouted Tom, setting off. He hoped he was helping Calvin but unfortunately he wasn't.

The boys began to cycle round the rec on the bumpy dirt path. Soon the other three began to leave Calvin behind. He could hear Robert calling "Come on, droopy bars" and this made him even more angry. His bike bumped and jarred on its thin racing wheels. It was built for speed on a smooth road, not for a rough track like this. The more Robert taunted him, the harder Calvin tried to catch up, until finally, inevitably, disaster struck. He hit a pot-hole, his front wheel collapsed and he flew through the air, landing on his back.

Within seconds the other boys had stopped and raced back to him. Philip asked if he was all right. Calvin stood up and brushed himself down. He was glad he had a helmet on when he felt the small dent on the back. He looked down at his mangled bike.

"I told you it was rubbish," said Robert.

"Shut up," snapped Tom.

"Yes, leave him alone," joined in Philip. They didn't really want to play with Robert. He always managed to be disagreeable in some way.

"He should get a decent bike," and with that parting shot Robert cycled away.

"He's right, it's a load of rubbish," said Calvin as he walked away, brushing off the tears.

"What about your bike?" called Tom.

"I don't want it," he shouted back and then he began to run. When he reached home he ran straight to his room before his mother could see him. Then he began to think about what he had done. He pictured his wrecked bike lying where he left it and wondered what he was going to tell his mum.

Some time later he went downstairs. His mother was sitting in the lounge, reading the paper. "Have a nice time on your bicycle?" she asked.

"All right," was all he could say. Then he noticed the bare corner in the lounge. "Where's the grandfather clock?" he asked.

His mother looked up from her paper. She hesitated before saying, "Even your second-hand bike was expensive, especially with the helmet as well. So I sold the clock to pay for it. I got a good price for it, so don't worry. I wanted you to have a really nice birthday."

Calvin couldn't believe what he was hearing. His mother had sold her most precious belonging so that he could have a bicycle, which was now lying in a heap at the rec. He didn't know what to say. Just then the doorbell rang. He went to answer it and there were Tom and Philip standing on the doorstep with his bike. Calvin was stunned: the bike looked as good as new.

"We were going to get you a joint birthday present, so we went to the cycle shop and got a new wheel for your bike," said Tom.

"The rest just needed adjusting," added Philip.

"What's this all about?" asked Calvin's mother as she came to the door.

Calvin was too overcome for words.

Discussion/Reflection

1. What do you think Calvin should tell his mother?
2. How do you think she will feel if she hears the truth?
3. What was the main reason for Calvin wanting a particular bicycle?
4. How did Calvin feel when he saw the racer?
5. How were Tom and Philip kind to him?
6. How did the grandfather clock play an important part in the story?
7. Have you ever wanted something really badly and not got it? How did you feel? How can you help others get over this feeling?

Prayer

Lord, teach us to remember that presents are often wrapped in love and that this wrapping lasts longer than the present. Amen.

Religious Links

The Tenth Commandment (Exodus 20:17) says, 'Don't covet anything that is your neighbour's.'

This story could be appropriate to use at Christmas time when we talk with children about giving and receiving gifts, or when celebrating Divali or other festivals involving the giving and receiving of presents.

Follow-up Activities

1. Ask the children to look up the word 'covet' in the dictionary. Would this be a suitable word to use for Calvin?
2. Ask the children to think of other things they would love to have but can't. Then ask them to think about a hungry child in a third world country and make a list of the things that child would love to have. The obvious point here is to show how privileged children in Britain are. This could be developed using poetry.

FEELINGS

9
The Dog

It was a warm, sunny day and the children wandered around aimlessly in the heat during lunch break. A few were lazily throwing a tennis ball to each other; rackets had been banned the day before because someone got hit on the head. Lakshmi and Lisa were sitting on the grass near the school pond making daisy chains.

Suddenly there was a commotion by the back gate. Children had gathered around to look at something. Lakshmi and Lisa got up and strolled over to see what was happening. As they approached the group, out stepped Calvin holding the collar of a very excited dog. It was a black and white border collie and it seemed to enjoy all the fuss it was creating.

"Is this your dog?" asked Lakshmi as she bent down to stroke it.

"No, Fly belongs to my neighbour. She's always getting out," replied Calvin.

"What are you going to do?" asked Lakshmi.

"I'll ask Mrs Jones if I can take her home," replied Calvin. But Mrs Jones said no, it was up to Fly's owner to come and collect her. So they tied the dog to the school fence and then telephoned Calvin's neighbour to come and collect her.

After the lunch break Mrs Jones called the register. It was then when they noticed that Lisa was missing.

"Does anyone know where Lisa is?" asked Mrs Jones.

"She was with me most of the lunch break," said Lakshmi.

"Shall I go and look in the toilets, Miss?" suggested Joanne.

"Yes, but be quick, we've a lot to do this afternoon."

Joanne left in search of Lisa and quickly came back. "Please, Miss, I've found her but she won't come out of the toilets."

Mrs Jones left the class and went to see what the problem was. She found Lisa locked in a cubicle, refusing to come out. She also refused to say what was wrong. Mrs Jones sent for Mr Hall, who arrived with a special key to open the locked cubicle. When they opened the door they found Lisa huddled in the corner, white as a sheet and clearly very frightened.

Mr Hall helped Lisa up and suggested that she should sit in the staff room for a while until she calmed down. But no matter how hard he tried, he could not get Lisa to explain to him what was wrong. Lisa remained quiet and her breathing became difficult as if she was going to have one of her asthma attacks. At this point Mr Hall decided to call her parents.

Mr Calder, Lisa's father, arrived in ten minutes with her asthma medicine but Lisa still said nothing about what was upsetting her. Then suddenly there was an excited barking outside as Fly's owner arrived to collect her. At the sound of the barking Lisa looked around worriedly and it was then that her father realized what had happened.

What do you think is wrong with Lisa?
How could someone become really frightened of dogs?

Mr Calder explained that when Lisa was three years old, one day a large dog suddenly ran out from a garden, knocked her over and bit her on the arm. Ever since then she had been terrified of dogs.

"Well, Lisa," said Mr Hall, "I wish you had told us all about this. We would have taken Fly right away from the school buildings."

Mr Calder took Lisa home, while Mr Hall explained to Mrs Jones and the class what had caused her to be so upset.

A few weeks later Mrs Jones announced that a blind lady was coming in to talk to the children about the work of the Royal National Institute for the Blind. She did not tell them that Mrs Chapman had a guide-dog; she wanted to keep this as a surprise.

When Mrs Chapman arrived she left Bonnie, her guide-dog, outside the classroom and Mrs Jones guided her to a seat in front of the class. She began to tell them what it was like being blind and what special things blind people needed around the house to help them. It was when Tom asked her about guide-dogs that Bonnie was introduced. Mrs Chapman called her name and in came a sleek golden dog with a waggly tail. Lisa was frightened and sat very still, but Mrs Jones had made sure she was sitting next to her and when Bonnie came in she was able to put an arm around Lisa and reassure her that everything was all right.

Mrs Chapman began to explain how Bonnie had been trained and how she was such an important part of her life. Mrs Jones could feel Lisa beginning to relax slightly. A little later, as Mrs Jones had suggested, Mrs Chapman asked if someone could fetch a drink of water for Bonnie.

Lots of hands went up but Mrs Jones said, "Perhaps Lisa would like to."

There was silence in the class as everyone looked at Lisa. Mrs Jones took her hand and helped her out of her chair. This was a moment Lisa would always remember. She stood there, looking at Bonnie, her heart racing and her breathing coming fast. She had a strong urge to run out of the classroom. If she had turned towards the door she would have seen her father looking anxiously through the glass.

"Here you are, Lisa," said Mrs Chapman as she held up Bonnie's bowl. "She would love a nice long drink."

Slowly Lisa walked to Mrs Chapman. There wasn't a sound in the classroom. All the children knew of Lisa's fear and were waiting to see what she was going to do. She took the bowl from Mrs Chapman, went to the sink and filled it. Then cautiously she took it to Bonnie. She stood in front of the dog and carefully placed the bowl on the floor. Bonnie began to drink, while Lisa stood watching, unable to move. Then suddenly, without warning, Bonnie looked up and licked Lisa's hand. Quickly Lisa drew her hand away but she continued to stand there. She could still feel Bonnie's wet tongue on her hand.

"That was a nice thank you kiss," said Mrs Jones, and as the class laughed quietly the tension seemed to lift.

"Lisa, why don't you stroke Bonnie," suggested Mrs Jones.

Lisa tentatively put out her hand and touched Bonnie's head. Bonnie licked her again and Mrs Chapman said, "I think she likes you, Lisa."

Lisa smiled at this. She had won.

Discussion/Reflection

1. What is meant by 'She had won'? What were Lisa's feelings when she was walking up to Bonnie and then afterwards when the dog licked her?
2. How do you know that Mrs Jones had deliberately arranged this?
3. When Lisa first stood up why was it a 'moment she would always remember'?
4. How did Lisa show bravery?
5. Why do you think Lisa couldn't explain her fear when Fly came into the playground?
6. Think about the things you are frightened of: it might be spiders, tests or heights. How could you try to overcome this fear?

Prayer

Let us pray for the strength we need to face difficult situations. We pray that our faith will never leave us. Amen.

Religious Links

Religions are about the faith their founders and heroes have had and the risks they've taken as a result. Can you think of one person in a religion you know about and the difference that having faith made to that person?

Follow-up Activities

Give children the opportunity to discuss their fears, in pairs or small groups, and then perhaps as a whole class. Some discussion points could be:

- How do fears originate?
- Are fears sensible (e.g. a fear of harmless creatures such as spiders)?
- What can we do to overcome our fears?
- What can we do to help others overcome theirs?

10
The New Coat

THEME: respect for other people's property

Joanne could hardly wait to get home to see if it had finally arrived. Her mother had ordered it from her latest catalogue and the delivery was promised for today. She opened the front door and there sitting on the telephone table was a large brown package. Dropping her bags, she eagerly picked it up and raced into the kitchen to find her mother.

"I see you found it then," said her mother, who was peeling potatoes ready for dinner.

"Can I open it?" Joanne asked.

"Of course you can, it must be yours. I've not ordered anything else lately," replied her mother.

Joanne got a pair of scissors and carefully slit open the package. She knew from past experience not to rip the bag open in case the order wasn't right and they needed to send it back. But a great smile came over her face as she drew out the pale mint-green coat. It was just as lovely as the picture in the catalogue. She quickly put it on and stood in front of the long mirror in the hall. It was perfect. It was a thick, warm winter coat with a furry-rimmed hood. The buttons down the front sparkled like gold and it had two deep pockets. It was the colour that attracted her – it would complement her long blond hair.

"Very smart," said her mother, standing behind Joanne as she hugged herself in front of the mirror. "I do wonder if you chose the right colour, though."

"Oh Mum, it'll be all right, I'll look after it." When they were discussing what colour to order, her mother wanted her to have a darker one that wouldn't show any dirty marks.

"Can I wear it to school tomorrow?" she asked.

"But we agreed that you would save it for best," said her mother.

"Oh please, I promise to look after it. Just for tomorrow, please?" pleaded Joanne.

Her mother saw how proud she was of her new coat. She really didn't want Joanne to wear it to school because it was expensive and all sorts of accidents could happen at school. Joanne's father was unemployed and they only had his benefit and her own wage from her part-time job at the bookshop to live on. The coat was really more than she could afford but she didn't want to disappoint Joanne.

"All right, but you must be careful!"

"Thanks, Mum. I can't wait till tomorrow." Joanne very carefully took off the coat, found a coat hanger and hung it on the back of her bedroom door. When she went to bed that night she lay there looking at it for ages before she turned off the light.

Why was Joanne so keen to wear her coat to school?
Why did her mother not want her to wear it?

The next day Joanne was up earlier than usual. She was pleased to see that it was a sunny day. If it had been raining, her mother might have made her wear her old anorak. Her plan was to prove to her mother today that she could be careful with her coat and then persuade her to let her wear it every day.

"What an early bird," said her mother, "I wonder what got you up at this time?" Joanne just grinned, she knew what her mother meant. "As you're up so early, you can help with the breakfast dishes before you go. There's no point in getting to school before anyone's there to admire you."

Joanne was bursting with pride as she walked to school, dressed in her new coat. She decided to be a bit later than usual to make sure all her friends were at school when she made her grand entrance. And she wasn't disappointed. As soon as she arrived, her friends gathered round, saying what a lovely coat it was and asking if they could try it on. Of course she didn't allow them to.

Before she went into class she made sure that her coat was safely hooked on her peg. She had often seen coats knocked on to the floor and accidentally trampled on by children hurrying outside.

At playtime she rushed out to the cloakroom, just to make sure that her coat was all right. Putting it on, she went outside but was disappointed to find that the day was beginning to warm up and many children were taking off their coats to play. Joanne decided to sit and watch: she didn't want to risk getting her coat dirty.

After play Joanne began to settle down to her work, the initial excitement about her new coat beginning to fade. When she had eaten her lunch, she put on her coat again to go outside, though most of the others didn't even bother to take theirs out. It was so warm that the boys were playing football just in shirt sleeves.

Come on, Joanne, let's practise shooting," called her best friend, Subatra. Mrs Jones usually allowed them to practise netball shooting during the lunch break.

Joanne wanted to take part as she watched the other girls. She looked around. No one was on the bench, so she took off her coat, carefully folded it up and put it on the clean bench. She didn't want to put it on the ground in case it got dirty. Then she joined in the netball practice.

Meanwhile the boys were choosing their football teams. Once organized, they set up their goals at either side of the playground, the goal posts usually being piles of discarded coats. They tried to pinch one of the netball posts but the girls shooed them

away. Calvin set up his goal with a couple of bins, while Tom was still looking around for something. He spotted a brick by the school fence and as he ran to pick it up he passed the bench and grabbed a pale green coat. Now he had his two goalposts. The game began and the ball whizzed about from one side of the playground to the other.

"Goal!" shouted Calvin's team, as he sent a shot through Tom's goalposts. The ball rolled off the playground into the wet grass. Tom ran after it, slipping a bit on the muddy ground. As he ran back he angrily kicked the coat on the ground and then placed the ball in the centre of the playground, ready to start the game again. It was at this point that a loud screech was heard which stopped everyone in their tracks and brought the dinner supervisors running.

Joanne stood there, staring down at her coat – her new pale mint-green coat that was now in a heap on the dirty playground. And worse – much, much worse – were the dark brown muddy streaks all over the back of it. She stood there, tears rolling down her face, unable to pick it up. Other children gathered around, the boys coming over to see what the fuss was all about.

"Joanne, what's the matter?" asked Mrs McEwan, one of the dinner supervisors.

"It's her coat, Miss," said Subatra, glaring at Tom who was standing there holding the football.

Mrs McEwan picked up the coat and said, "Thomas, it looks as if you have been using this as a football."

"No, Mrs McEwan, we only used it as a goal post," he replied.

"Did you ask Joanne if you could use her coat?"

"No, but we always use coats," he said.

"Why didn't you use your own?" Mrs McEwan asked.

"We didn't bring ours out. It was only for a few minutes. It's only a coat," protested Tom.

"Well, it isn't your coat, it belongs to someone else. I think you had better explain all this to Mrs Jones." With that she led Tom into school, carrying a very grubby coat and with a tearful Joanne being comforted by Lisa close behind.

Because Joanne was so upset, Mrs Jones telephoned her mother who came and collected her. She wasn't very pleased with Joanne but she didn't say much; after all, she told herself, it wasn't really Joanne's fault. But she was still very annoyed.

So were Tom's parents. Mrs Jones contacted them as well and suggested that Tom should pay for the coat to be cleaned. It cost him four weeks' pocket money.

Joanne's coat looked as good as new when it came back from the cleaners but somehow it didn't feel as good as new when she put it on. Of course, now she only wore it for best.

Discussion/Reflection

1. At the end of the story why do you think Joanne no longer felt that her coat was as good as new?
2. How did Tom show a lack of respect for other people's property?
3. Did Joanne look after her coat properly? What were her feelings when she saw her coat lying dirty on the ground?
4. How could she have avoided all this trouble?
5. Was it Joanne's mother's fault for giving in to her?
6. Tom took something which did not belong to him, without asking. How would you feel if someone did that to you?
7. If someone took or borrowed something that belonged to you and broke it, would you feel angry?

Prayer

Let's try to be still in God's presence. [A silent pause.] Lord, we want people to be careful with things that are precious to us. May we be careful with things that are precious to them. Amen.

Religious Links

Matthew 7:12 says, 'Whatever you want people to do for you, do for them: this sums up the religious law and the teaching of the prophets.'

Follow-up Activities

An interesting issue for the children to debate could be whether Tom's action in taking Joanne's coat was stealing. What is stealing? Is it simply taking something that does not belong to you, or does there have to be an intention not to give back?

11
Joey and Flo

THEME: facing up to responsibility

Joey and Flo were two guinea pigs. Mrs Jones had decided to do a project about pets. This was very popular with those who had pets, but those who didn't felt a bit left out. That's where Joey and Flo came in; they belonged to Mrs Jones's own children but she brought them to school so that everyone in the class could learn about looking after pets.

There was a great sense of excitement when she brought them in. The children put some tables together and Mrs Jones carefully put the two little animals in the middle. She asked her class questions about what guinea pigs eat and how they should be looked after. The children watched the animals with fascination and there was uproar when Joey left a puddle on Philip's Maths book.

Once all the children had stroked them – except for Lisa, who was allergic to them – Mrs Jones put the guinea pigs back into their hutch. They were going to look after the animals for the duration of the project, about three weeks, and so Mrs Jones asked for volunteers. Of course, lots of hands shot up but when she asked all those who already had a pet at home to put their hands down she was left with twelve hands still up. She divided those twelve children into three groups of four – one group for each week. It was their job to feed and exercise the guinea pigs and clean out the hutch.

The timetable worked well at first. The first group spent every spare minute playing with the animals. The children refilled the water, looked for fresh dandelion leaves and cut up bits of carrot and lettuce for them. They exercised them on the grass, usually with hordes of other children looking on, and they cleaned out the hutch at the end of the week. The second group worked well too, though there were fewer children watching – the novelty had worn off by then.

Tom, Calvin, Joanne and Subatra made up the last group. The problem was they could not get on with each other; they always argued. So they decided to look after the guinea pigs in pairs – the boys on Monday and Thursday, the girls on Tuesday and Wednesday, and then all of them on Friday, the day for cleaning out the hutch.

All went well until Thursday. It was a lovely sunny day and the boys raced outside to play football after lunch. Mr Hall had said they could go on to the grass because it was dry, which meant they could have a decent game of football for once. Half-way through the game Tom suddenly remembered the guinea pigs. He looked around and saw Calvin at the far end of the field. They were having a good game and he didn't want to leave it. He was torn about what to do when he saw Joanne and Subatra walking along the edge of the field. He called them over and asked if they could feed the guinea pigs and they said yes. Feeling happier, Tom returned to the game.

As the girls set off towards the hutch, Mr Bell approached them. He asked if they could help him sort out some musical instruments. They didn't know what to say because they knew they should feed the guinea pigs but they did like Mr Bell and would prefer to help him. They spotted Lisa sitting on a bench doing nothing and ran up to her. Subatra asked her if she could feed the guinea pigs and before Lisa realized what she was saying she agreed. Joanne and Subatra ran off to join Mr Bell, shouting out thanks over their shoulders.

All four children have passed on their responsibility to someone else, but what have they forgotten about Lisa?

Lisa stood there, wondering what to do. She had kept away from the guinea pigs so far because of her allergy. Her mother had told her not to go near them. But she longed to stroke them and she was envious of the others who were allowed to play with them. She walked slowly past the hutch. She had often done so before and had had no reaction. Maybe guinea pigs had a different kind of fur that wouldn't affect her. She decided to take a chance.

She picked some dandelion leaves from the edge of the field and when she had a handful she went to the hutch. She also took two carrots from a bag, then she carefully opened the door of the hutch. Joey and Flo squealed with delight because they knew it was their feeding time. They came to the door of the hutch and Lisa stroked each in turn, delighting in the touch of their soft, warm little bodies. She had just put the food into their dish when suddenly she started to sneeze and sneeze and sneeze. She realized sadly that she was very allergic to guinea pigs!

Lisa was still sneezing as she went into school and her eyes were running. Mr Hall saw her and asked what was the matter. She said it was the pollen in the air which had started her hay fever off. He told her to have a rest indoors out of the warm spring air.

At the end of the day Tom and Calvin thought that Joanne and Subatra had looked after the guinea pigs. Joanne and Subatra thought Lisa had looked after them but they had forgotten about Lisa's allergy. When her sneezing started, Lisa had forgotten to close the hutch door properly. That night Joey and Flo discovered a new freedom they didn't expect.

The next morning found Mrs Jones's class in despair. The guinea pigs were nowhere to be seen. The children looked everywhere, frantically calling and whistling. They searched around the trees, in the hedges and behind the P.E. shed. Suddenly, Robert came running up to Mrs Jones, shouting something about the school pond. Several children were already gathered around the pond, staring into it. There, floating quite still, was Joey. He must have tried to have a drink but fell in and drowned.

The children were very upset. Tom and Calvin turned on Joanne and Subatra, saying that they had offered to look after the guinea pigs. The two girls glared at Lisa and said she was to blame. Lisa burst into tears; she was very distressed and blamed herself.

When she eventually found out exactly what happened, Mrs Jones consoled Lisa, telling her she wasn't really to blame. She was very angry with the other four; she told them that it had been their responsibility to look after the guinea pigs and they should not have put Lisa in that situation. The children were silent – they could make no excuses.

There was still no sign of Flo. Throughout the day the search for her continued. They decided that she must have escaped under the fence into someone's back garden. Some of them said they would go round at the weekend and ask to search in the gardens. They were very worried that Flo might get run over by a car or even caught by a cat.

It was a long weekend, especially for the four disgraced children. On Monday morning they were all eager to find out if there was any news.

With a solemn voice, Philip announced that he had found Flo. He went out to the cloakroom and came back carrying a small box. The children were quiet as he put the box down and opened the lid. There was a great sigh of relief when they heard her familiar squeaking noise. But as they peered into the box they saw not only a very lively Flo but three tiny baby guinea pigs! Philip had found them all on Sunday afternoon, in the very last garden he had searched.

There were two female babies and one male. The children unanimously decided to call the male one Joey. It seemed only right. The whole class had learned a very important lesson about taking their responsibilities seriously.

Discussion/Reflection
1. What lesson do you think they learned?
2. Do you think it was fair that the children blamed Lisa?
3. How did the other children feel about the guinea pigs' escape?
4. Why didn't Tom and Calvin look after the guinea pigs properly? How did they feel when they realized what had happened?
5. Why did Lisa lie about her sneezing?
6. How do you feel when you do a job badly and you let someone else down?
7. How do you feel when someone lets you down? Can you trust them when you ask them to do something again?

Prayer
Let us ask God for strength to carry out all our responsibilities, even if we do not like them. Help us through these difficult moments so that we shall learn courage, perseverance and trust. Amen.

Religious Links
In the Bible, the story of Jonah is about someone trying to get out of a job God wanted him to do. Jonah was frightened and did not ask God for help. As a result he had an alarming adventure with a large fish! This story would make a good subject for a dramatic presentation in assembly.

Follow-up Activities
1. Having a pet is a responsibility. Discuss the needs of pets and how different pets are looked after.
2. Look at the responsibilities children have at home and at school. Discuss the consequences if they are not handled well.

12
The Best Gift

THEME: giving without expecting anything in return

Lakshmi was a very popular girl in the class because she was always kind and friendly. She would readily lend her felt-tips to others and she was usually the first to show concern if someone was unhappy. So when she came to school one day, not her usual cheerful self but quiet and preoccupied, everyone was surprised.

"What's wrong with you this morning?" asked Lisa, Lakshmi's best friend.

Lakshmi turned to her and asked, "Would you like to buy my pens?"

Lisa was taken aback for an instant, "No, I've got enough. Why do you want to sell them?"

"I need to get some money," replied Lakshmi. Then she explained to Lisa about elderly Mrs Bevan. Lakshmi visited her every Friday on the way home from school. She enjoyed telling her all about her week at school and Mrs Bevan gave her a cup of tea and a biscuit. It was only a short visit but both of them enjoyed it. Now it was Mrs Bevan's birthday tomorrow and Lakshmi wanted to buy her something nice but she didn't have any money. She didn't want to ask her parents. The Chatterjis ran a small fruit and vegetable shop and business was a bit quiet at the moment.

"Do you think your dad will give you a bag of fruit to take her?" suggested Lisa.

Lakshmi looked doubtful, "I don't know, he might do, but it's not very much to take."

That evening Lakshmi decided to ask her mother for a small bag of fruit to take to Mrs Bevan. Her mother thought that it was a very nice idea and she put some apples and oranges in a bag for her. "Don't tell your father. He'll say we're giving away his profits," she said.

After school the next day Lakshmi knocked on Mrs Bevan's door. The elderly lady opened the door with her usual welcoming smile. "Come in, come in, my dear. I've put the kettle on ready."

"Happy birthday, Mrs Bevan," said Lakshmi as she came inside.

"Fancy you remembering it's my birthday today," said Mrs Bevan.

"I've brought you these. I wanted to buy something better, but ..."
"Oh, my dear, you didn't have to give me anything," said Mrs Bevan.
"But I wanted to give you a present for your birthday," replied Lakshmi.
"Listen, Lakshmi, you give me a wonderful gift every week," said Mrs Bevan.
Lakshmi looked at her, puzzled. She didn't know what Mrs Bevan meant.

Discussion/Reflection

1. What did Mrs Bevan mean? How did Lakshmi's visits make her feel?
2. Why was Lakshmi a popular girl in the class?
3. Why did Lakshmi enjoy going to see Mrs Bevan?
4. Do you know someone you could visit and brighten up their day?

Prayer

All the world's great religions stress the importance of caring for others. In silence let us think what we can do to help. If you feel able, use the pause to ask for God's blessing on forgotten people who are lonely and perhaps sad or afraid.

Religious Links

Throughout his teachings Jesus talked about how we should give to and help each other. The hymn 'When I Needed a Neighbour' is a good illustration and mirrors Matthew 25:31–46. Luke 14:12–14 looks at the theme of giving to those who cannot give back.

The Qur'an teaches Muslims to remember the poor at all times. In particular, the festival called Eid ul Fitr, at the end of Ramadan, is a time for thinking about the poor. The help given need not be money but can be friendship and practical help.

Follow-up Activities

1. Many children have elderly relatives. Discuss aspects of old age, such as loneliness, and the need for elderly people to look after themselves properly. What do elderly people contribute to the community?
2. Groups of children could list ways of helping elderly people, such as doing shopping for them in bad weather, keeping them company, walking their dog.
3. What other groups of people in the community would benefit by children giving up some time for them? How could the children help?

13
It Was Only an Accident

THEME: forgiveness

Robert was standing outside Mr Hall's office. He often found himself there because he had a short temper and was always lashing out with his hands or feet. But this time he was really worried. They had been playing football and he accidentally kicked the ball in the wrong direction; it smashed through a classroom window. Mrs McEwan, the dinner supervisor, sent him in to Mr Hall. Now Robert was waiting for the headteacher to finish his telephone call.

"Come in," said the voice inside.

Robert walked into the office and stood in front of Mr Hall's desk.

"I've just been on the telephone to the glaziers to get them to repair your handi-work," said Mr Hall. "Well, what have you to say for yourself?"

"It was an accident, Mr Hall," explained Robert. "I didn't mean to kick the ball like that."

The headteacher looked hard at Robert. He could see that the boy was worried, not his usual confident self. He decided to give Robert the benefit of the doubt. "All right, I'll forgive you this time. If you say it was an accident then I'll believe you," he said. "Go on, you can carry on with your game but you must be more careful. Perhaps you should play further away from the school."

Robert was greatly relieved. He ran out to the playground to join the others. Soon he was running after Philip, who had the ball. Philip saw him coming and, in a desperate hurry to get rid of the ball before he was tackled by the oncoming Robert, kicked it as hard as he could in the direction he was facing. Unfortunately the ball flew up and hit Robert full on the face. He fell to the ground with a loud shriek.

Philip ran over to him anxiously. "Are you all right? I'm sorry, I didn't mean to kick the ball at you."

Robert stood up and glared at Philip, "You did that on purpose."

"I didn't," protested Philip. "It was only an accident."

"Oh yeah? Well, this is going to be an accident as well," snarled Robert, as he pushed Philip over. He raised his foot to kick him when a loud voice boomed across the playground.

"You two, come here!" shouted Mr Hall who had been out to inspect the broken window.

Robert and Philip walked over to him. "What's going on?" asked Mr Hall.

"He kicked the ball straight into my face on purpose," accused Robert.

"I didn't," said Philip. "It was an accident."

"It wasn't!" argued Robert.

The other boys had wandered over to listen. "Calvin and Tom, did you see what happened?" asked Mr Hall.

"It was an accident, like Philip said," replied Calvin.

"Yeah, the ball just flew up," agreed Tom. "He didn't kick it at him on purpose."

Mr Hall turned to Robert. "I think we had better have another talk – about forgiveness. Come on, into my office again."

Discussion/Reflection

1. Philip said sorry to Robert when he accidentally kicked the ball into his face but what was Robert's reaction?
2. What do you think Mr Hall is going to say to Robert?
3. Have you ever done something wrong to someone? Was it deliberate or an accident? Would you have felt better if they had forgiven you?

Prayer

Forgive us our wrongdoings as we forgive the wrongdoings of others.
Amen.

Religious Links

1. In Matthew 18:21–35, Peter asks Jesus how many times he should forgive someone who sins against him. Jesus replies by telling the story of the servant who owed money to his master. Eventually the master showed compassion and forgave him his debt. The servant in turn was owed money but, instead of forgiving, he had the debtor thrown into prison. When his master found out, he was very angry.
2. Jewish new year is the start of a period of ten days when people look back over the last year. They remember things they have done wrong and try to put them right. They say 'sorry' and ask for forgiveness.

Follow-up Activities

1. Children could discuss whether or not Robert should be punished. What is the best way for Robert to learn his lesson?
2. Discuss the difference between forgiving someone for something done accidentally and forgiving someone for something that is deliberately done.
3. Saying 'sorry' can be a very difficult thing to do. What are some of the things children might be sorry for? What ways are there of 'saying sorry'? (Related activities can be found on page 61.)

14
A Friend in Need

THEME: friendship

Mrs Jones began calling the register. When she got to Joanne's name there was no answer.

"Does anyone know where Joanne is?" she asked the class. "Subatra, do you know?"

"No, Miss," came the reply. Subatra thought Joanne must be ill. She was usually at school before her and she hadn't mentioned going anywhere today.

Subatra soon forgot about Joanne's absence because that morning she had to go to the dentist. Her mother was coming to pick her up at ten o'clock and then they had to catch a bus to the other side of the town.

As the bus slowly made its way through the town centre, Subatra gazed out of the window. Suddenly her attention was caught by a group of girls outside a shop. Three were teenagers but the fourth was younger – it was Joanne. She wasn't with her mother and she wasn't wearing her normal school clothes. She must have stayed away from school without her parents knowing.

Subatra was puzzled. She had heard Joanne talk about a new girl in her street who was at the senior school. Was Joanne missing school to be with her?

The trip to the dentist was soon over and Subatra was glad to be on the way back to school. From the bus she watched the crowds closely but she saw no sign of Joanne. She began to wonder if it had really been Joanne she saw.

After school she decided to take a short detour and pop into Joanne's house. Mrs Mitchell answered the door. "Hello, Subatra. I'm afraid Joanne's not back from school yet. Do you want to come in and wait for her?"

Subatra didn't know what to say: Joanne's mother evidently thought she was at school. Just at that moment Joanne herself walked up the path. She was wearing her school uniform. When she saw Subatra and her mother at the front door she hesitated for a moment.

Subatra could see the look of panic on Joanne's face, so she took a book out of her bag and said, "You left one of your books behind on your desk. Mrs Jones asked me to give it to you."

"Oh, thanks," said Joanne, the panic disappearing. "Do you want to come in?"

"No, I must go, I promised Mum I'd be home straight after school," replied Subatra, turning away.

When Subatra got to school the next day, Joanne was there waiting for her. "Thanks for not telling my Mum that I wasn't at school yesterday," she said.

"I saw you in town when I went to the dentist. What were you doing?" asked Subatra.

Excitedly, Joanne began to tell her all about it. When she left home, instead of going to school, she went to Heather's house. Heather was the new girl in her street. She changed her clothes and then they caught a bus into town and met up with two of Heather's friends. They spent the day looking round the shops. Outside a record shop the three older girls told Joanne to wait for them while they went inside. When they came out a few minutes later, to Joanne's delight they handed her a tape of her favourite group. This was the only thing the girls bought, except for a bag of chips at lunchtime.

"You can imagine how I felt when I saw you talking to my mum," finished Joanne. "Thanks for not telling on me."

"But Jo, you're going to get into real trouble if anyone finds out, especially your mum," said Subatra.

"Don't be daft, we won't choose the same day each week," replied Joanne.

"You're not planning to go again?" said Subatra in disbelief.

"Why not, it was a laugh. It doesn't hurt anyone." Joanne spoke defiantly.

"But it's deceitful, you're supposed to be at school," said Subatra.

"You're a wimp," taunted Joanne and with that she flounced off.

Subatra was upset: Joanne was her best friend and she knew she was being led astray by those older girls but she didn't know what to do.

The girls didn't speak much during the next few days. Then came the morning that Subatra feared. Joanne didn't turn up at school.

Subatra has got a problem. If she tells someone, then Joanne will blame her for getting her into trouble, but if she doesn't tell, then Joanne could end up in even worse trouble. What would you do?

Subatra worried about Joanne all morning. During the lunch break Mrs McEwan, one of the dinner supervisors, said to her, "You look a bit glum today. Where's your friend?"

Subatra liked Mrs McEwan. She was a large, friendly, cuddly sort of person, just the kind to confide in. So Subatra began to tell her about Joanne and how worried she was that Joanne was being led into trouble by the others.

"You realize I'll have to tell Mr Hall about this?" Mrs McEwan said when she'd finished. Then, in answer to Subatra's look of panic, "Don't worry, I'll not say who told me." She left Subatra wondering if she had done the right thing.

The next morning Joanne arrived at school with her mother and both went straight in to see Mr Hall. Later, when Joanne came into the class she shot a hostile look at Subatra. Of course, Mr Hall didn't say who had told but Joanne could guess.

All day Joanne ignored Subatra. She didn't even give her friend a chance to explain. Subatra felt thoroughly miserable; she wanted to talk to Joanne about it.

It was almost time to go home when Mr Hall came into the classroom and asked Joanne to come to his office. There, waiting with her mother, was a policewoman. On the desk was the tape that Heather had given Joanne the week before. That afternoon Heather and her two friends had been caught stealing tapes. They had said that Joanne had also been involved.

Joanne burst into tears and tried to tell them her side of the story. The more she tried to explain, the more she realized how stupid she had been to trust Heather.

Unlike Heather, Joanne had never been in trouble before. Mr Hall told the police-woman that Joanne was a very good pupil and he believed her when she said she knew nothing about how the other girls got the tapes. The policewoman decided to take no action about Joanne but gave her a warning about making friends with the wrong sort of people.

By the time they had finished, all the children had gone home. But as Joanne and her mother left the school there was one person left. There, by the gate, was Subatra, waiting to walk home with her friend.

Discussion/Reflection

1. Who was the real friend to Joanne – Subatra or Heather?
2. When did Subatra first help Joanne?
3. Do you think that Subatra did the right thing in telling Mrs McEwan? What were Subatra's feelings about this?
4. What lessons do you think Joanne has learned? How would she feel when she saw Subatra outside by the gate?
5. Which friend would you rather have? Which kind of friend are you?

Prayer

Let us ask for God's help to be loyal and true to our friends through good and bad times, never to be afraid to admit we are wrong or to say sorry. Amen.

Religious Links

John 15:13 says, 'The greatest love a person can have for their friends is to give their life for them.' Children could research real life examples of this, e.g. Captain Oates on Scott's last polar expedition.

Follow-up Activities

1. Children could discuss the qualities of a true friend. They could make a list of their friends. They may have more than they realize: teachers and other adults at school, the police, neighbours and so on.
2. In groups, children could make up a short play about a quarrel between friends and show how the quarrel was resolved.
3. Resolving quarrels usually means that someone has to say 'sorry'. Children could explore the importance of this word. (Related activities can be found on page 57.)

15
The Swimming Pool

THEME: perseverance

It was the moment Philip had been dreading – class J's turn to go swimming. In fact it was their third trip this term but he had been 'ill' on the two previous occasions. When he complained of a stomach-ache this morning his mother realized what he was doing and took him to school herself. The problem was he couldn't swim. He was the only one in the class who couldn't and he felt embarrassed about it. He saw his mother speaking to Mrs Jones, which made him feel even worse!

At the pool the children were grouped according to ability. Another class teacher took the better swimmers and Mrs Jones took the rest. Philip was one of the last to get changed. Tom could see him hanging behind in the changing room.

"Come on, Philip, it's great fun," coaxed Tom.

"I don't want to," said Philip, trying to keep the tears back. "I can't swim."

"Well, that's the whole point of coming here," said Tom. "Anyway, you're not the only one."

Philip looked at him hopefully. "Who else can't swim?" he asked.

"Subatra, Joanne and I are the best swimmers. Calvin splashes about a bit but he can get across the pool. Lakshmi got rid of her floats last week but Marie still can't really swim," said Tom.

This made Philip happier as the two of them walked into the pool area, though the strong smell of the chlorine made him wrinkle his nose. Tom went off to the top group and Philip enviously watched him dive into the water to join the others who were already swimming across the pool. He walked over to Mrs Jones who was handing Marie a pair of floats. Other children were jumping in and trying out their strokes. His first two fears quickly vanished: nobody teased him and he wasn't the only one who couldn't swim.

How did Tom help Philip overcome his nervousness?
Do you think Philip's mother was cruel taking him to school that morning?

Mrs Jones helped Philip into the pool. He was surprised how warm the water was. And it was not very deep at this end, only up to his chest. Mrs Jones took him through a series of activities that involved getting his shoulders and head under the water. At first he didn't like it but once he realized that he wasn't going to sink to the bottom and also that Mrs Jones was right there to help him, he soon began to relax and almost enjoy himself. Next he was given two floats and told to try following Marie across the pool.

"Come on, Philip, this is good fun," called Marie as she boldly kicked across to the other side, supported by her floats. It took most of the lesson for him to get his feet off the bottom but in the end he succeeded. It was with great disappointment that he heard the whistle blow for the end of the session.

"Well done, Philip," said Mrs Jones, as he climbed out of the pool. "I'm very pleased with you. We'll have you swimming like a fish in no time."

Philip was delighted. He'd not only survived the swimming lesson, he'd actually enjoyed it! Tom came over and asked him how he got on.

"Great," replied Philip, "I can't wait till next time."

Philip didn't have another stomach-ache. With each session he gained in confidence and he really worked hard. Very soon he used only one float, then just had one hand on the float while he paddled with the other hand. After two more sessions he didn't need a float at all and he took his first few unaided strokes. Now he set himself a new target – to swim the full width of the pool by the end of term.

Discussion/Reflection

1. What were Philip's feelings about swimming at first?
2. What did he try to do to get out of swimming?
3. How did other people help him get over his fears?
4. Philip worked very hard to learn to swim. What were his feelings at the end of the story?
5. Think about a time when you were frightened about doing something. It might have been swimming, like Philip, or reading something in assembly, or playing an instrument in front of an audience for the first time. What were your feelings before and after your experience? Did anyone help you through it?
6. How could you help others overcome their fears?

Prayer

Lord, teach us to learn. Help us to overcome our fears. Amen.

Religious Links

The word 'disciple' means a student or a learner. In the great world faiths disciples are rarely super-heroines and heroes, but ordinary people who gradually learned to take the risks of faith and were happier for it.

Follow-up Activities

1. The children can discuss things they have had to work hard at. It could be school work, a sporting activity, or a personal quality such as controlling their temper. They can talk about their worries and how they succeeded.
2. Discuss the support others give to help us get over our difficulties. Why are praise and encouragement so important?
3. How do we learn a skill? Talk together about the type of training, equipment and practice needed.